Y0-AUZ-852

Taking EARTH'S Temperature

CLIMATE CHANGE AND Food Production

Jodie Mangor

Rourke
Educational Media

rourkeeducationalmedia.com

Before & After Reading Activities

Before Reading:

Building Academic Vocabulary and Background Knowledge

Before reading a book, it is important to tap into what your child or students already know about the topic. This will help them develop their vocabulary, increase their reading comprehension, and make connections across the curriculum.

1. Look at the cover of the book. What will this book be about?
2. What do you already know about the topic?
3. Let's study the Table of Contents. What will you learn about in the book's chapters?
4. What would you like to learn about this topic? Do you think you might learn about it from this book? Why or why not?
5. Use a reading journal to write about your knowledge of this topic. Record what you already know about the topic and what you hope to learn about the topic.
6. Read the book.
7. In your reading journal, record what you learned about the topic and your response to the book.
8. After reading the book complete the activities below.

Content Area Vocabulary

Read the list. What do these words mean?

acidic

conversion

crops

emissions

environments

politics

precipitation

species

supplemental

sustainable

After Reading:

Comprehension and Extension Activity

After reading the book, work on the following questions with your child or students in order to check their level of reading comprehension and content mastery.

1. What are some of the ways climate change could affect food production? (Summarize)
2. If the ocean becomes too acidic for plankton to form and grow, how could this affect the human food supply? (Infer)
3. How will rising temperatures affect the ability of livestock to provide us with food? (Asking Questions)
4. What effect, if any, has climate change had on the food you eat? (Text to Self Connection)
5. What are three food choices we can make to help limit climate change? (Asking Questions)

Extension Activity

Choose an unprocessed food you are interested in (a fruit, grain, vegetable, fish, or simple livestock product). Research what it needs to grow and how climate change might affect this food. Then have an adult help you prepare a meal that contains this food.

TABLE OF CONTENTS

CHAPTER ONE

FEEDING THE WORLD

Imagine a classic American-style breakfast: eggs, toast with butter, orange juice, and bacon. And don't forget the coffee or tea. Where did each of these items come from? How far did they need to travel to reach your plate?

With modern transportation, the world's food supply has become more interconnected than ever before. Still, about one in nine people do not have enough to eat and the global population continues to grow. Scientists predict that to feed everyone, farmers will need to double the amount of **crops** they produce by 2050. Climate change is going to make it difficult to reach this goal. That's because the main food sources for people around the world—crops, livestock, and fish—are sensitive to climate.

Climate change is expected to affect agriculture around the world.

*Weather and climate: what's the difference? Weather is the daily state of the atmosphere around us. It includes factors like temperature, **precipitation**, humidity, and wind. Climate is the average of weather conditions in an area over time. A place with a dry climate can still have days of rainy weather.*

All of our food sources are closely linked to their **environments**. As the climate changes, farmers may need to adjust what crops they grow, and where and when they grow them.

The same hot weather that is good for limes and other citrus fruit makes kale and spinach bolt and taste bitter.

There is a lot of evidence that Earth's climate is changing. The global average temperature is increasing. Precipitation patterns are changing. Glaciers are melting, oceans are warming and becoming more *acidic*, and sea levels are rising. Extreme weather events, such as droughts, fires, and flooding, have become more common.

It could also become more difficult to raise animals. Dry spells, drought, and heat waves are hard on livestock. Warmer weather could lower the quality of their feed. As water temperatures rise, fisheries will also be affected.

Cattle and pigs eat less when under heat stress.

Climate change is already affecting our food supplies. But the amount and quality of food we produce doesn't depend on climate alone. Farming practices, new technology, and even **politics** also come into play. People's beliefs affect our government policies and how we do business.

1.2 trillion

Effects of climate change cost the world 1.2 trillion dollars per year.

There is an overwhelming amount of scientific evidence that human activities are a major cause of climate change. But not everyone wants to accept this. Some industries and politicians do not want to take inconvenient steps that might limit economic growth now, for benefits that will only show up sometime in the future.

How farms fare in the future depends on all of us. By educating ourselves about climate change and the effects that farming practices have on the environment, we will be able to make informed choices going forward.

If everyone in the U.S. gave up meat one day a week, the national greenhouse gas emissions would be reduced 0.6 percent.

CHAPTER TWO

CROPS

Weather has always affected agriculture. Scientists are predicting quicker and more extreme changes in temperature and precipitation. Some places will benefit, at least at first.

More Frost-Free Days: Longer U.S. Growing Season

10

5

Long-term Average
0

-5

1895   1925   1950   1975   2015

CLIMATE CENTRAL

Deviation from average days, based on frost-free season
Source: EPA/Kunkel, 2015

Overall, the growing season in the U.S. is increasing.

Frost-Free Season is Getting Longer
Change in Annual Number of Days

+16
+10
+10
+19
+9
+6

Frost free season is the period between the last below 32°
Reading in the spring and the first in the fall. 1991-2012 period relative to 1901-1960.
Source: National Climate Assessment 2014

CLIMATE CENTRAL

The growing seasons of northern countries such as China, Canada, and Russia are expected to become longer and warmer. But other places, like Brazil, the Midwestern United States, and Eastern Australia, will become too hot or dry for many crops.

Projected impact of climate change on agricultural yields

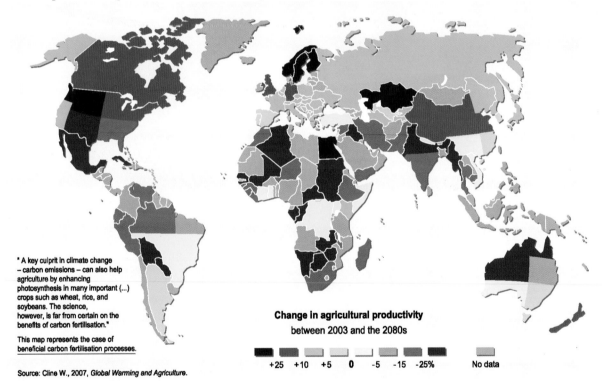

* A key culprit in climate change – carbon emissions – can also help agriculture by enhancing photosynthesis in many important (...) crops such as wheat, rice, and soybeans. The science, however, is far from certain on the benefits of carbon fertilisation."

This map represents the case of beneficial carbon fertilisation processes.

Source: Cline W., 2007, *Global Warming and Agriculture.*

Change in agricultural productivity
between 2003 and the 2080s

+25 +10 +5 0 -5 -15 -25%   No data

Hotter temperatures will make it more difficult for farmers to work. This will lead to less food production. The human population is expected to grow most in the tropics. This is also where agriculture will be hardest hit by climate change.

Each crop **species** grows best in a certain temperature range. Rising temperatures could have a number of effects. Farmers may be able to expand where they grow some crops, such as melons and sweet potatoes. Warmer temperatures and longer growing seasons could lead to higher yields.

New York State was once too cool to grow soybeans, but in 2013, farmers planted a record amount.

Scientists are developing new varieties of crops that can grow well in warmer, drier climates.

But many other crops, including grains and soybeans, do not grow well or produce good quality seed if the temperature increases even by a little bit.

Many fruit trees need a certain amount of time in the cold to produce a good crop. In California, winters are warmer, and almond, cherry, and apricot trees are producing less than before. To compensate, farmers might be able to plant new varieties that need fewer chill days, but this would take a lot of time and money.

Climate change is connected to rising levels of carbon dioxide (CO_2) in our atmosphere. More carbon dioxide in the air may help rice, soybean, and some other crops grow faster. But it can create conditions that harm plants.

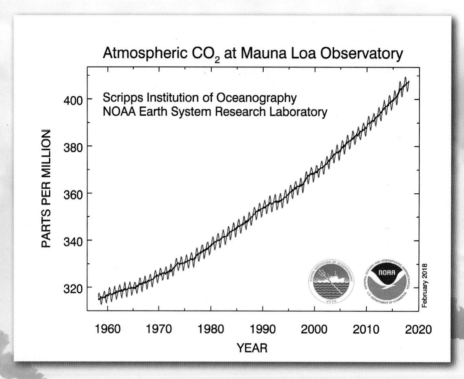

The amount of carbon dioxide in the atmosphere has increased over the past 60 years.

Carbon dioxide is a common, colorless, odorless, natural greenhouse gas. It traps the energy from the sun and keeps the world at a livable temperature. Burning fossil fuels and other human activities have increased the amount of carbon dioxide in the atmosphere, trapping more heat than before.

Crops grown in the presence of more carbon dioxide have lower levels of important nutrients such as protein, nitrogen, zinc, and iron. Researchers haven't yet figured out why higher levels of carbon dioxide cause crops to lose nutrients.

Climate change is a serious risk to crops in sub-Saharan Africa and other places with little water.

Forestland, prime agricultural land

Savanna/Scrub, prime pasture, suitable farmland

Grassland, suitable pastoral land

Semi-desert, suitable for camels

Extreme desert, practically uninhabitable

Africa, Present Day

More than 70% of African farmers rely on rain to grow crops.

It takes 1,320 gallons (4,997 liters) of water to produce what an average American eats in a day.

Seventy percent of the Earth's available freshwater is used for agriculture. Climate change is affecting rainfall patterns. Heavy rainfalls and drought conditions are becoming more common. Both extremes can destroy crops. Heavy rain can delay planting, increase root diseases, cause floods, and wash away fertile topsoil. Droughts dry out topsoil, so it is more likely to blow or wash away.

EFFECT OF CLIMATE ON PLANT GROWTH

Environmental conditions play a big role in how well a plant can grow over time. This experiment will take two weeks.

YOU'LL NEED:

- Six small plants (all the same variety, roughly the same size)

- A large, clear container with a lid or top

- Water

DIRECTIONS:

1. Divide the plants into three groups of two.

2. Label the first group "control." Keep these plants at room temperature and water them daily.

3. Label the second group "drought." Keep these at room temperature too, but do not add any water to the container for six days. Water normally for two days and then stop watering again for another six days.

4. Label the third group "heat." Place these plants inside the clear plastic container, cover and place on a warm windowsill. Let the temperature inside the container rise to above 95 degrees Fahrenheit (35 degrees Celsius). Grow the plants in this environment for 14 days, watering daily.

5. Each day, write down what you see. Note how tall the plants are, how many new leaves they have, and whether the plants are wilting. How does each condition affect plant growth?

CHAPTER THREE

LIVESTOCK

Around the globe, people keep cattle, sheep, pigs, goats, chickens, and other livestock to supply meat, milk, and eggs. Livestock provide the world's population with 25 percent of its protein.

Over the past 20 years, meat and egg production have risen by well over 100 percent.

Livestock do more than supply food. They can be fed damaged fruit, grains, and household wastes. They can reduce weeds in coconut, oil palm, and rubber plantations. In many places, they are a source of power and transportation. Their manure is valuable too—as fertilizer, or a source of fuel.

About 75 percent of cropland in the U.S. is used to grow feed for livestock.

Seven pounds (3.18 kilograms) of plant protein plus 6,000 gallons (22,712 liters) of water = one pound (0.45 kilograms) of beef.

Animal products offer several advantages over crops as a source of food. Livestock can turn unusable plant material into high-value milk and meat. Milk can be preserved as butter or cheese, and meat can be dried, salted, or smoked. But raising livestock uses up a lot of resources and creates pollution, including greenhouse gases.

To thrive, livestock need to live in an environment that doesn't get too hot or too cold. They also need enough water. But climate change will increase the risk of extreme weather that can cause livestock stress. During heat waves, animals don't eat as much. That means they produce less meat, less milk, and fewer eggs.

At high temperatures, chickens lay smaller eggs that break more easily.

As temperatures rise, animals may be less healthy, grow less, and have fewer young. All this means they may provide people with less food. At high enough temperatures, animals can die.

Scientists expect pork, beef, and milk production to decrease with warming temperatures.

More than a quarter of Earth's
land is used for livestock grazing.

As temperatures rise, many weeds
are expanding where they grow.

Many weeds grow faster than field crops.

Already, scientists think increased temperature, decreased rainfall, and higher levels of carbon dioxide have changed pastureland. It is lower quality, with more weeds that animals don't eat. This leads to lower production of animal products. One solution is to give pasture-raised cattle more **supplemental** feeds.

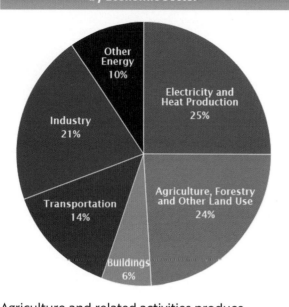

Global Greenhouse Gas Emissions by Economic Sector

- Other Energy 10%
- Electricity and Heat Production 25%
- Industry 21%
- Agriculture, Forestry and Other Land Use 24%
- Transportation 14%
- Buildings 6%

Agriculture and related activities produce more greenhouse gases than all our cars, trucks, trains, and airplanes combined.

Some people believe that raising livestock contributes to climate change, and that we should consume less meat and dairy. Others disagree.

Most of the increase in greenhouse gases over the past 150 years has been caused by human activities.

The livestock industry produces about 15 percent of the greenhouse gas **emissions**. Cows, pigs, and goats release methane. This gas absorbs 25 times more solar energy than carbon dioxide.

30
to
236

Depending on its diet and whether it's producing milk, a cow can emit anywhere from 30 to 236 gallons (114 to 893 liters) of methane daily.

Adding dried seaweed to a cow's diet can reduce methane emissions by 70 percent or more.

GETTING GASSY

Aside from being affected by global warming, agriculture also contributes to the problem. Cattle and rice farms produce methane gas. Fertilized fields release nitrous oxide. Rainforests release carbon dioxide when they're cut down to grow crops or raise livestock. These gases trap heat in the atmosphere.

CHAPTER FOUR

FISHERIES

Oceans cover about 70 percent of the Earth's surface. The world's fisheries provide an important source of protein to at least half the world's population. But that may not always be so. Fisheries are already stressed by overuse and pollution.

The oceans are a major source of food.

Arctic and freshwater species who live far north will have nowhere cooler to go.

Ocean ecosystems are very sensitive to changes in the climate. As the Earth's climate gets warmer, the ocean—and the life in its waters—will change. Fish are expected to decrease in number and size, and move toward Earth's poles, where it is cooler. Some fish will go extinct.

The ocean can absorb large amounts of heat without a large increase in temperature. More than 90 percent of the warming from the past 50 years has been in the ocean. Its ability to store and release heat helps stabilize the Earth's climate system.

Ocean Heat Content, 1955–2015

Ocean heat content (10^{22} joules)

- NOAA ➤
- MRI/JMA
- 1971–2000 average
- CSIRO

Year: 1960, 1970, 1980, 1990, 2000, 2010

Oceans have become warmer since 1955.

Hundreds of millions of people depend on fishing to make a living.

Still, rising temperatures can cause changes in sea levels, ocean currents, and dissolved oxygen levels, which in turn can result in large fluctuations in fish stocks.

The ocean also absorbs extra carbon dioxide from the atmosphere. The more carbon dioxide the ocean absorbs, the more acidic its water becomes. If it gets too acidic, animals such as clams and mussels can't form their shells. Lobsters are threatened by shell disease. Some plankton can't form properly. Plankton are an important part of the ocean's food web. Many fish and animals, including some whales, depend on plankton to survive.

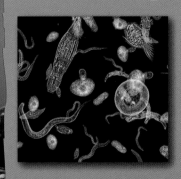

Phytoplankton are tiny organisms that are an essential part of the ocean food web. Like plants, they turn sunlight and carbon dioxide into food and oxygen, and are the first link in many food chains. A huge number of fish and other animals depend on phytoplankton for their survival.

SHELLS IN ACID

As the ocean absorbs more carbon dioxide, it is becoming more acidic.

YOU'LL NEED:

- Two clear drinking glasses
- White vinegar
- Water
- Two pieces of the same type of seashell

DIRECTIONS:

1. Place a piece of shell into each glass.

2. Cover one of the shells with white vinegar. This is the acid.

3. Cover the other in water.

4. Check the glasses every morning and evening for two to four days. Compare what is happening to each shell.

Why do shells break down in acid?

Shells are mostly made of calcium carbonate, a base. When the acid in the vinegar comes into contact with the calcium carbonate, a chemical reaction occurs. Bubbles of carbon dioxide are released as the shell breaks down. Ocean water isn't as acidic as the vinegar in this experiment, but can still affect sensitive shell-building animals.

WHITE VINEGAR

CHAPTER FIVE

PESTS OF PLANTS AND ANIMALS

Weeds, insects, and other disease-causing organisms cause up to 25 to 40 percent of all crop losses. Many of these pests benefit from the wetter climates and increased carbon dioxide levels that climate change may bring.

Some crop pests are becoming more difficult to manage.

Increasing temperatures help many pests develop and reproduce more quickly. With fewer freezing winters to keep them in check, we can expect more of these pests, in more places. This will lead to greater crop losses.

Southern pests such as the corn earworm are expanding north.

In the southeast United States, kudzu is an aggressive weed. It has invaded 2.5 million acres (one million hectares) and could move north into agricultural areas.

Climate change may allow weeds to grow faster than field crops. Weeds reduce food yield. Weeds compete for light, nutrients, and water, interfere with harvesting, and act as hosts for insects and other disease-causing organisms.

Extreme weather events can wipe out many insect eggs and larvae.

Around the world, weeds cause the most crop losses.

Pesticides are used to keep them in check. But these chemicals can be expensive, and bad for water quality and human health.

Many of the pests that make livestock sick are thriving, thanks to earlier springs and warmer winters. When it's dry, animals cluster together more often at waterholes. Disease spreads more easily, and because animals are stressed they are more likely to get sick.

Climate change is leading to a rise in livestock diseases.

Affected animals produce less meat and wool.

midge

Bluetongue is one example of a disease that is expanding its range. This disease causes sheep, cattle, and goat tongues to swell and turn blue. It is caused by a virus from Africa and Southeast Asia. The virus is spread by a tiny biting insect called a midge that likes a warm and wet climate. The disease was recently found in Western Europe. It has killed more than 1.5 million sheep there.

CHAPTER SIX

DISTRIBUTION AND TRANSPORT

Chances are, all the food on your breakfast or dinner plate has passed through many hands before reaching you. Farmers, transporters, food processors, and stores all play a part.

Food supplies around the world are interconnected. International trading in food is on the rise. In many countries, nearly 70 percent of food comes from somewhere else. Bananas are one of the largest fruit crops of the world. Yet they only grow in tropical climates. Banana plants need 10 to 15 frost-free months to produce a flower stalk.

Bananas are eaten in at least 192 countries, on every continent.

Climate change affects how much food can be produced. Agricultural crops, livestock, and fisheries are all affected.

Agriculture in North America hasn't been affected by temperature and precipitation changes as much as in other places. The U.S. produces as much as 40 percent of the world's corn and soybeans. It also produces a lot of wheat. These amounts may need to increase to meet the world's needs.

Temperatures above a certain level can cause food yields to drop.

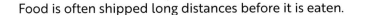

Food is often shipped long distances before it is eaten.

Climate change also affects our ability to move food where it needs to go. Extreme weather events caused by climate change can disrupt food delivery. This can result in food shortages and higher food prices. Increasing temperatures can cause food to spoil before it reaches people's mouths.

Producing food contributes to greenhouse gases. All in all, food production could account for as much as 30 percent of emissions. Growing, processing and transporting, land **conversion**, and storing wasted food are all activities that contribute.

Sustainable agriculture produces food using farming methods that protect the environment.

To help limit climate change, we need to find ways to make food production more **sustainable** with fewer emissions.

What Can We Do?

We can start by making good choices about what we eat.

- Buy foods with minimal or no packaging.

- Eat more plant-based foods.

- If meat is a part of your diet, consider eating less, especially red meat. Raising beef cattle requires 28 times more land than raising pigs or chickens, 11 times more water, and produces five times more greenhouse gas emissions.

- Eat local foods that don't have to be transported long distances.

What's the difference between organic and nonorganic foods? Organic foods are grown with only natural substances. Nonorganic foods may be grown with industry-made chemical fertilizers or pesticides. It generally takes less energy to grow organic foods, but they cost more. Fruits and vegetables grown by either method can be part of a healthy diet.

What we eat can help decide
the future. We could add up to
50 percent more calories to the
world's food supply by eating more
crops instead of feeding them
to livestock. We could also take
steps to reduce food waste, since
25 percent of the world's food is
thrown out instead of eaten.

Glossary

acidic (uh-SID-ik): acid-forming

conversion (kuhn-VUR-zhuhn): a change of something into something else

crops (krahps): plants that can be grown and harvested

emissions (i-MISH-uhns): substances released into the atmosphere

environments (en-VYE-ruhn-muhnts): the natural surroundings of living things

politics (PAH-li-tiks): competition between groups or individuals for power and leadership of a country, state or city

precipitation (pri-sip-i-TAY-shuhn): water that falls to Earth as rain, sleet, hail, or snow

species (SPEE-sheez): a category of living things that can mate and produce offspring

supplemental (suhp-luh-MENT-uhl): added to something to make up for what is missing

sustainable (suh-STAY-nuh-buhl): done in a way that can be continued and that doesn't use up natural resources

Index

Show What You Know

1. What are the three main food sources for people around the world?

2. How do climate and weather differ?

3. Name three ways climate change is affecting the fishing industry.

4. In what ways could climate change have a negative effect on raising livestock?

5. In which areas of the world will agriculture be most affected by climate change?

Further Reading

Carmichael, Lindsey, *How Can We Reduce Agricultural Pollution?*, Lerner Classroom, 2016.

Pollan, Michael, *The Omnivore's Dilemma: Young Readers Edition*, Dial Books, 2015.

Lee, Blair, *The Science of Climate Change: A Hands-On Course*, Secular Eclectic Academic, 2017.

About the Author

Jodie Mangor writes magazine articles and books for children. She is also the author of audio tour scripts for high-profile museums and tourist destinations around the world. Many of these tours are for kids. She lives in Ithaca, New York, with her family.

www.rourkeeducationalmedia.com

PHOTO CREDITS: istock.com, shutterstock.com, Cover: corn © Subbotina Anna, lettuce © Tortoon, eggs © N-sky, hen © l i g h t p o e t; PG4; Fudio. PG5; Andrius Kaziliunas, Leonid Eremeychuk, zakaz86. PG6; oticki, twildlife, NolanBerg11, impr2003, BenGoode. PG7; Taglass, Page Light Studios. PG8; KatarzynaBialasiewicz, anyaivanova. PG9; Ekkasit919, songqiuju, ddsign_stock. PG10; cossmix, kavram, standret. PG11; Cline W. (GWA), EPA -Kunkle, CC National Climate Assessment. PG12; rottadana, AndreaAstes, Givaga, LysenkoAlexander. PG13; YanLev, THANATASDcom, dionisvero. PG14; mapichai, NOAA, JM_Image_Factory. PG15; Zzvet. PG16; Dmytro Shestakov, knowlesgallery, Sohadiszno. PG17; Sohadiszno, obewon, SilverV, Hyrma, Chepko. PG18; GlobalP, Bestgreenscreen, Chalabala. PG19; Jevtic, robynmac. PG20; SW_Photo, fotojv. PG21; Patarapong, Easy_Asa PG22; savoilic,Tashka, EKramar. PG23; PicturePartners, 2windspa. PG24; rrodrickbeiler. PG25; JohnCarnemolla, VietNamVui, vovashevchuk, GlobalP. PG26; Tanjulchik, Baloncici. PG27; vlad61, randimal. PG28; vlad61, gianliguori. PG29; twildlife. PG30; carlosrojas20, chengyuzheng, bonchan, EddWestmacott. PG31; prill, akinshin. PG32; fotokostic, dimid_86. PG33; eskymaks, Patipas. PG34; VR_Studio, GlobalP. PG35; wasja, Shtrunts. PG36; PhillipMinnis, Rasica. PG37; robbinsbox, Ian_Redding. PG39; zhudifeng, erierika, Saisampankaye. PG40; Rasica, fotokostic, Biletskiy_Evgeniy, Yasonya, UrosPoteko. PG41; lloydmp, ChristinLola. PG42; VanderWolf-Images, OlyaSolodenko, Ralph125. PG43; Harlequin129, sezer66. PG44.45; Rawpixel, Wavebreakmedia, 3sbworld

Edited by: Keli Sipperley

Produced by Blue Door Education for Rourke Educational Media. Cover and Interior design by: Jennifer Dydyk

Climate Change and Food Production / Jodie Mangor
(Taking Earth's Temperature)
  ISBN 978-1-64156-450-2 (hard cover)
  ISBN 978-1-64156-576-9 (soft cover)
  ISBN 978-1-64156-694-0 (e-Book)
Library of Congress Control Number: 2018930477

Rourke Educational Media
Printed in the United States of America, North Mankato, Minnesota